A: The worst?

B: The absolute worst

A: There is lots -of them. Socks, clothes... One year a friend literally bought me a screw so I could "Screw my head on"

B: Wow.

A: So someone actually gave me an insult as my birthday present.

B: So is that the worst?

A: No! The following year the same person told me he was going to give me my life's worth.

B: Ok?

A: And the 'friend' just did this (drops five cent coin into B's hand)

B: Wow. Who did this?

A: You don't need to know. (Points and glares at a random audience member.

And Scene

2

A: What's your favorite smell?

C: (Quietly) Lawn clippings.

A: Awh, that's ok.

B: Have you been. Here before?

C: Not this particular one, the one done the street though.

A: Your in for a treat

(A and B count down from 3, hitting zero they open the car doors. They all moan in delight a smell hits their nostrils.)

A: Mmm. Breathe it in

B: So good!

C: Yes! (they moan as they are pushing the air in towards them)

B: No no! Stop! (pushes C's arm down as A shuts the doors)

A: Be careful.

B: You're still a virgin.

A: Oh shoot, mums coming, one more go?

(B and C nod, A and B open the cars doors, moaning like earlier, until mum appears at the door)

B: Oh hi mum! Did you use the premium diesel?

Everyone but mum: That $1.50 extra really hits the spot.

And Scene

3

(Requires group of 10.)

(8 members become a big tree, the

other 2 are lovers)

A: I love you.

B: I love you more.

A: I loved before I met you.

B: I loved you before you were born.

A: You know what we should do?

B: Carve our names into that tree?

(The tree's stump starts shaking no, as the lovers dig their knife it the tree, all 8 peoples face scrunch up then)

Tree: *Screaming* Why would you do that! You monster! What is wrong with you! I hope you break up!

A and B: Sorry!

(A and B run off, lights dim)
And Scene

4

A: She's going to like this *laughs a bit*

(A pulls pants out a bit and takes a pic of the inside of his pants. He snapchats it out)

B: Son/Daughter, we need to talk with you.

(Parents walk in)

C: Yes, we do

(Dads phone dings with a new snapchat)

A: Don't open that!

Lights Cut Out to Black

And Scene

5

(All actors in scene placed around the room randomly)
(One by one, every time they say a line, they get lit up)

A: World Peace

B: To end inequality

C: To rid world hunger

E: A big boat

F: Snapchat filters in real life

G: Pizza for every meal, but stay healthy.

H: Real life purge

I: My parents to figure out if they still love each other. I don't care if they divorce, well I do. But I want them to put all of us out of our misery.

E: Like, a really, really big boat!

J: LESS FRIENDS

E: A gigantic boat. Wait no! The Titanic!

And Scene

6

(Titanic theme playing in the background, 2 actors as Rose and Jack, rest are making a boat)

R: Its beautiful!

J: I know, isn't it?

R: I'm flying Jack, im flying!

J: Wait, somethings missing.

(Everyone creates a huddle, point at 3 people individually, 3 actors go and get the audience members and place them like an ice berg, then reset to ship)

R: Oh Jack! I love!

(The ship moving forward during their lines, once the tip slightly touches the iceberg, wait 3 seconds. All actors scream as the boat sinks.)

Return audience to seats

And Scene

7

EXT. A SUPERMARKET – AFTERNOON

Friendly Shop Keeper DR ROBERT COX is arguing with

incredible gardener MS NADINE JEMALL. ROBERT tries to hug NADINE but she shakes him off.

ROBERT

Please Nadine, don't leave me.

NADINE

I'm sorry Robert, but I'm looking for somebody a bit more brave. Somebody who faces his fears head on, instead of running away.

ROBERT

I am such a person!

NADINE frowns.

NADINE

I'm sorry, Robert. I just don't feel excited by this relationship anymore.

NADINE leaves.

ROBERT sits down, looking defeated.

Moments later, bold Unemployed MS ALICE GREENFIELD barges in looking flustered.

ROBERT

Goodness, Alice! Is everything okay?

ALICE

I'm afraid not.

ROBERT

What is it? Don't keep me in suspense...

ALICE

It's ... a villain ... I saw an evil villain terrorise a bunch of elderly ladies!

ROBERT

Defenseless elderly ladies?

ALICE

Yes, defenseless elderly ladies!

ROBERT

Bloomin' heck, Alice! We've got to do something.

ALICE

I agree, but I wouldn't know where to start.

ROBERT

You can start by telling me where this happened.

ALICE

I was...

ALICE fans herself and begins to wheeze.

ROBERT

Focus Alice, focus! Where did it happen?

ALICE

a book shop! That's right - a book shop!

ROBERT springs up and begins to run.

EXT. A ROAD - CONTINUOUS

ROBERT rushes along the street, followed by ALICE. They take a short cut through some back gardens, jumping fences along the way.

EXT. A BOOK SHOP - SHORTLY AFTER

JEMMA WILLIAMS a scheming villain terrorises two elderly ladies.

ROBERT, closely followed by ALICE, rushes towards JEMMA, but suddenly stops in his tracks.
ALICE
What is is? What's the matter?
ROBERT
That's not just any old villain, that's Jemma Williams!

ALICE

Who's Jemma Williams?

ROBERT

Who's Jemma Williams? *Who's Jemma Williams?* Only the most scheming villain in the universe!

ALICE

Blinkin' knickers, Robert! We're going to need some help if we're going to stop the most scheming villain in the universe!

ROBERT

You can say that again.

ALICE

Blinkin' knickers, Robert! We're going to need some help if we're going to stop the most scheming villain in the universe!

ROBERT

I'm going to need paper, lots of paper.

Jemma turns and sees Robert and Alice. She grins an evil grin.

JEMMA

Robert Cox, we meet again.

ALICE

You've met?

ROBERT

Yes. It was a long, long time ago...

EXT. A PARK - BACK IN TIME

A young ROBERT is sitting in a park listening to some reggae music, when suddenly a dark shadow casts over him.

He looks up and sees JEMMA. He takes off his headphones.

JEMMA

Would you like some jelly tots?

ROBERT's eyes light up, but then he studies JEMMA more closely, and looks uneasy.

ROBERT

I don't know, you look kind of scheming.

JEMMA

Me? No. I'm not scheming. I'm the least scheming villain in the world.

ROBERT

Wait, you're a villain?

ROBERT runs away, screaming.

EXT. A BOOK SHOP - PRESENT DAY

JEMMA

You were a coward then, and you are a coward now.

ALICE

(To ROBERT) You ran away?

ROBERT

(To ALICE) I was a young child.
What was I supposed to do?

ROBERT turns to JEMMA.

ROBERT

I may have run away from you then,
but I won't run away this time!

ROBERT runs away.

He turns back and shouts.

ROBERT

I mean, I *am* running away, but I'll be
back - *with paper*.

JEMMA

I'm not scared of you.

ROBERT

You should be.

INT. A SWEET SHOP - LATER THAT DAY

ROBERT and ALICE walk around searching for something.

ROBERT

I feel sure I left my paper somewhere around here.

ALICE

Are you sure? It does seem like an odd place to keep deadly paper.

ROBERT

You know nothing Alice Greenfield.

ALICE

We've been searching for ages. I really don't think they're here.

Suddenly, JEMMA appears, holding a pair of paper.

JEMMA

Looking for something?

ALICE

Crikey, Robert, she's got your paper.

ROBERT

Tell me something I don't already know!

ALICE

The earth's circumference at the equator is about 40,075 km.

ROBERT

I know that already!

ALICE

I'm afraid of sausages.

JEMMA

(appalled) Dude!

While JEMMA is looking at ALICE with disgust, ROBERT lunges forward and grabs his deadly paper. He wields them, triumphantly.

ROBERT

Prepare to die, you scheming carrot!

JEMMA

No please! All I did was terrorise a bunch of elderly ladies!

NADINE enters, unseen by any of the others.

ROBERT

I cannot tolerate that kind of behaviour! Those elderly ladies were defenceless! Well now they have a defender - and that's me! Robert Cox defender of innocent elderly ladies.

JEMMA

Don't hurt me! Please!

ROBERT

Give me one good reason why I shouldn't use these paper on you right away!

JEMMA

Because Robert, I am your mother.

ROBERT looks stunned for a few moments, but then collects himself.

ROBERT

No you're not!

JEMMA

Ah well, it had to be worth a try.

JEMMA tries to grab the paper but ROBERT dodges out of the way.

ROBERT

Who's the mummy now? Huh? *Huh?*

Unexpectedly, JEMMA slumps to the ground.

ALICE

Did she just faint?

ROBERT

I think so. Well that's disappointing. I was rather hoping for a more dramatic conclusion, involving my deadly paper.

ROBERT crouches over JEMMA's body.

ALICE

Be careful, Robert. It could be a trick.

ROBERT

No, it's not a trick. It appears that... It would seem... Jemma Williams is dead!

ROBERT

What?

ROBERT

Yes, it appears that I scared her to death.

ALICE claps her hands.

ALICE

So your paper did save the day, after all.

NADINE steps forward.

NADINE

Is it true? Did you kill the scheming villain?

ROBERT

Nadine how long have you been...?

NADINE puts her arm around ROBERT.

NADINE

Long enough.

ROBERT

Then you saw it for yourself. I killed Jemma Williams.

NADINE

Then the elderly ladies are safe?

ROBERT

It does seem that way!

A crowd of vulnerable elderly ladies enter, looking relived.

NADINE

You are their hero.

The elderly ladies bow to ROBERT.

ROBERT

There is no need to bow to me. I seek no worship. The knowledge that Jemma Williams will never terrorise elderly ladies ever again, is enough for me.

NADINE

You are humble as well as brave!

One of the elderly ladies passes ROBERT a magical ring

NADINE

I think they want you to have it, as a symbol of their gratitude.

ROBERT

I couldn't possibly.

Pause.

ROBERT

Well, if you insist.

ROBERT takes the ring.
ROBERT
Thank you.

The elderly ladies bow their heads once more, and leave.

ROBERT turns to NADINE.
ROBERT
Does this mean you want me back?
NADINE
Oh, Robert, of course I want you back!

ROBERT smiles for a few seconds, but then looks defiant.
ROBERT
Well you can't have me.
NADINE
WHAT?
ROBERT
You had no faith in me. You had to see my scare a villain to death before

you would believe in me. I don't want
a lover like that.
NADINE
But...
ROBERT
Please leave. I want to spend time
with the one person who stayed with
me through thick and thin - my best
friend, Alice.

ALICE grins.
NADINE
But...
ALICE
You heard the gentleman. Now be off
with you. Skidaddle! Shoo!
NADINE
Robert?
ROBERT
I'm sorry Nadine, but I think
you *should* skidaddle.

NADINE leaves.

ALICE turns to ROBERT.
ALICE
Did you mean that? You know ... that
I'm your best friend?
ROBERT
Of course you are!

The two walk off arm in arm.

Suddenly ALICE stops.
ALICE
When I said I'm afraid of sausages,
you know I was just trying to distract
the villain don't you?
THE END

8

A: Your always on that thing.

B: You take everything for granted

A: Just because im friends with a guy, doesn't mean he's my boyfriend.

B: You young ones are all the same

A: Hooligans

B: Money doesn't grow on tree

A: When I was your age…

B: Not all of us are attached to our phones

A: I used to walk 6 kilometers to school, you won't even walk up the driveway

B: Have you ever opened up a book?

A: We never had phones, internet, or even air-conditioning.

B: They don't care for anyone else but themselves.

A: What is a MEME!

And Scene

9

(6 actors and 6 audience members needed)

A: I am the (interrupted by a phone call)

(A answers the phone)

A: It's the director, can you please play my part while im gone, its easy, just read the highlighted parts. (Passing his script to an unsuspecting audience member)

B: Oh crap, I left my burrito in the microwave. (B walks up to audience member and gives script)

B: Can you read the highlighted parts for me? I'll be back in a second.

C: Crap, that was his?! (says what B said and runs off)
D: Oh no! (E is having an asthma attack and D and E run off)

All audience members chosen are one stage and read this.

A: I'm the protagonist

B: I'm the antagonist

C: I'm the lover

D: I'm in love with the lover

E: (Hits D) You said you loved me!

AND SCENE

THANKS FOR READING

This Book Wouldn't Be Possible
Without the Support of My Drama
Group.

Left Over Pickles Are Your Mum's
Best Friend.

So a special thanks to them for helping
me write/use some of their plays.
Hopefully I can write more to release to
the public, so they can perform our
plays.